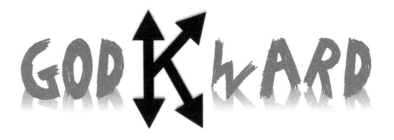

GOD KWARD

Finding Purpose in My Journey from Addiction into Recovery

Adam McMahan and Sean Joseph

ISBN 978-1-64191-055-2 (paperback)
ISBN 978-1-64191-056-9 (digital)

Christian Faith Publishing, Inc.
832 Park Avenue
Meadville, PA 16335
www.christianfaithpublishing.com

Printed in the United States of America

Godkward is dedicated to my loving wife, Lindsey,
and my children, Mackenzie and Grady.
In loving memory of Doug
May God's will continue to precede our own.

God·kward

/god-kwərd/

Adjective:

1. The presence of God amid a difficult or hard to deal with situation

   I didn't think I had the strength to endure watching my baby suffer through the treatments, but by the end of his stay, I realized just how Godkward my experience had been.

2. A situation that causes embarrassment and inconvenience best navigated with the guidance of the Holy Spirit

   When asked to speak about my sobriety in front of the church, I knew it would be Godkward; however, I was eagerly awaiting God's blessings for obeying Him.

INTRODUCTION

Addiction is an intimidating opponent, and people don't like to lose. That's why many addictions go unchallenged. Addicts become accustomed, even comfortable, with their habit. Substance abuse can feel so impossible to leave behind that some people ask, "Why should I have to? Stronger people than me have fought that battle and lost." The desire to change is critical, and sometimes that takes a catalyst.

God is calling you to face your opponent, leave your addiction behind, and follow Him. Yes, it's Godkward (the meaning of which we will dig into deeper soon), but He has a purpose for your life that will serve and advance His Kingdom. God needs your whole, healthy, and dedicated heart so you can serve the capacity and purpose He has for you—yes, even you. How do I know?

> *For God saved us and called us to
> live a holy life. He did this, not*

> *because we deserved it, but because*
> *that was his plan from before the*
> *beginning of time—to show us*
> *his grace through Christ Jesus.*
> *(2 Timothy 1:9, NLT)*

I wish we could open up the Bible and find a story about addiction and recovery. God didn't give us the story of an addict, though. However, He did provide us with truths throughout the Bible that apply to defeating formidable opponents. As I've drawn strength from the Bible during my own battle with alcoholism, I've noticed some parallels between my journey and a few of the classic characters: David, Peter, and Saul. If you're unfamiliar with these stories, it's worth your time to put this book down, pick up a Bible (or even your phone), and read them to lay a foundation before you continue. You can find the battle of David versus Goliath in 1 Samuel 17. Peter's Godkward experience of jumping ship to walk the water with Christ happens in Matthew 4. God exclaims His will to use and convert Saul to Paul, and the story of Saul's blinding journey happens in Acts 9.

God had a purpose for each of these men. He has a purpose for each of us too. The key is to listen to what He has asked us to do: Believe. Believe that what you hear Him calling for you to do is His will. Believe that He will deliver you from the hands of your addiction. Believe that He has a greater purpose for your life. Believe that the bad things happening are happening for a reason—His reason. He knows where you are and what has happened. Our purpose will unfold, in time, but first believe.

Before I share my story of recovery, I want to lay out the truths I've discovered in these Bible stories that make me confident that anyone can conquer addiction with God on his or her side. First, God can and will use anyone to advance His Kingdom. Second, David, Peter, and Saul all had problems, just like you and me, that would have made them think of themselves as unlikely to be chosen by God for anything. Third, what God called these Biblical heroes to do was the hardest thing they had ever done. Finally, and it may seem obvious yet it's worth pointing out, all of them listened.

1. God can use anyone.

David was a lowly shepherd boy whom God put at the right place at the right time. He had learned to use a sling as a weapon to fend off hungry predators from his flock. Little did he know that his skill would be used to slay Goliath. I'm sure David didn't realize he would become the main character in the most repeated metaphorical story of "the underdog" in history. That's what we addicts are, underdogs. We are in a fight to which we didn't consciously commit. How can we be brave and courageous and have faith? If we believe God will deliver us, as He did David, then we have faith.

Peter was a fisherman. I would imagine he smelled and cursed like the proverbial sailor too. When Jesus first saw Peter in his boat, He used an analogy for Peter to understand saying, "Come, follow me, and I will make you a fisher of men." What is your profession? I'd bet God has the ability to show you an analogy of how you can use it to advance His Kingdom.

Saul was a soldier—a mercenary, in fact. He was out and about killing Christians in the Roman Empire when Jesus used direct force to put an end to that violence. He simply told Saul it was over, that he had a new boss. Little did he know, while out killing Christians and forcing them to flee for their lives, that he inadvertently spread Christianity throughout the known world. The church grew because of his work against it. Believe it or not, as terrible as Saul's actions were, God used it for a purpose.

Are there some horrible things you've done that you feel you could never turn away from? Perhaps you feel like your flaws limit your purpose. I stand to reason that God has already used your character defects in a way that you just haven't seen yet. Why not seek Him out to find out what's next?

The point here is not that you have to be a commoner or a rebel for God to use you. The point is that God can use anyone, and you are someone! You don't go unnoticed if you're simply a social drinker. Certainly, you don't have to overdose for God to notice you. He already has. You don't have to compare your journey to anyone else's journey, standards, or skill set. God knows the special talents He gave you, and He intends to use them for His purpose.

Don't wait for the "right time" to start your battle against addiction. Time will expire. Don't wait to be in a better position in life; we aren't guaranteed tomorrow. Don't wait to become something you're not, because God desires to use you just the way you are.

2. *They all had problems.*

In fact, God has a proven track record of adopting and using people with problems some would consider more severe than addiction.

David was the runt. He was the youngest of eight brothers. He always had to do the grunt work out in the fields. His own father even forgot about him out with the sheep when Samuel asked Jesse to gather all his sons. Talk about family issues.

David's life did not become perfect after he slayed the mighty giant. Years later, after he became the king of Israel, he committed adultery, knocked up his mistress, and plotted to have her husband offed! Don't believe it? You can read all about it in 2 Samuel 11. *What a journey!*

Peter also made some major transgressions, and they were during Jesus's final hours, no less. Luke 22:54–62 explains how an angry mob caused Peter to leave his Savior hanging. Jesus was being taken to prison before the crucifixion, and people in the crowd accused Peter of being His follower. Peter, so shaken by fear, denied even knowing Jesus right to his face!

Before Paul became the face of the early Christian church's expansion, he was Saul, the face of its persecution. Saul witnessed and condoned the stoning of Stephen, a notable martyr, in Acts 7 and 8. He was a devout Jew who rocketed through the ranks by finding and arresting early followers of the Way. He had a hatred toward Christ, His followers, and anything that threatened the Jewish customs in their time.

There are so many more stories like these in the Bible. The people in them range from thieves to prostitutes, and God used all of them. He *uses* all of us. My story is proof that He still reveals His purpose to common folks with common problems. You can't hide your problems from God and He doesn't want you to try. In fact, He calls us to boast in our weakness.

> *Each time he said,* My grace is all you need. My power works best in weakness. *So now I am glad to boast about my weaknesses, so that the power of Christ can work through me. (2 Corinthians 12:9, NLT)*

Fight your addiction and don't hide your past. This is evidence that God wants to use the pain and struggles that you have gone through.

3. *It was the hardest thing they ever had to do.*

While David was confident God would deliver him from Goliath, I can't imagine he anticipated the persecution he would face afterward. I mean picture it. You've just "saved the world!" You are the hero! But your name has gotten too big. The very king whose country you saved now wants you dead. Jealousy is an ugly monster. Keep in mind when you begin to do the right things, the road gets narrower and narrower and the terrain more challenging. The enemy knows when you're up to something good, and he will use his powers to try and bring it to a halt.

Peter, after questioning Jesus, decided to be brave and take a step out of the boat. The dude walked on water. Jesus asked him to come. One condition was that Peter must keep his focus on Jesus. That had to be difficult. Guess what. The storm started booming, the sea was getting choppy, and Peter did the best thing that could have happened: He messed up. He took his eyes off Jesus. When he did, he sank. Jesus, of course, saved him. I picture myself often as Peter—sitting on the boat, wrapped in a towel, and soaking wet from my inadvertent swim, knowing I have just blown it. And then I smile, because immediately after making the mistake, Jesus saved me. He does that, and always will, should we let Him.

Saul, literally blinded by the truth, had to do a 180-degree turn. We as addicts will at some point reach an impasse that will require us to make an about-face. Saul was so well known for his murderous ways that he had to change his name to Paul. But the people knew there was more to his transformation. They saw it in how he spoke and how he carried the message of Jesus Christ. His actions were notable. Are you looking for something or someone to help you with your turnaround? I'm not saying you should change your name, but perhaps change the way you speak, change the things you speak about, and watch how your actions start to make believers out of those you've hurt in the past.

My journey to recovery is the hardest thing I have ever had to do, and yours will likely yield similar feelings. But you will begin to understand the value of making the daily, selfless sacrifice when you start buying into the purpose your Higher Power has for you.

4. *They listened.*

Maybe you're struggling to relate to these men from the past. If you're struggling to make the decision to quit, there is still something you can take away from these stories: They all listened to God. Those Biblical battles relate to yours because you are actually listening already. You're reading this book, aren't you? You are looking for validation and wanting a change. It's time.

Imagine if David declined Goliath's challenge. What would have happened if he returned to his sheep?

What if Peter stayed on his boat?

What if Saul continued to persecute Christians?

No King David, no St. Peter's Basilica, a lot fewer books in the *New Testament*—that's legacy lost, but God had a plan.

The reality is, though, it would have been easy for any of them to go about their daily lives like nothing happened. They could have chalked up their experiences with God as emotional highs, something they might act on later, or something they weren't prepared for yet. After all, everybody expected them to be who they already were, anyway. No one expected them to change: David the shepherd, Peter the fisherman, and Saul the soldier. Only God expected greatness out of them. Don't let what people expect out of you influence your actions. God knows His will for you.

How many times have we said "no" to God because of what other people thought? What has God revealed to you that you've come up with excuses not to do? Maybe you haven't always listened to Him before, but it is never too late to start. Life is about the journey!

My hope is that you draw strength from these stories just like I have. God didn't just work in people's lives during Biblical times. It humbles me to reflect on how many connections my story has with these and others in the Bible. He made heroes out of David, Peter, and Saul. He has made a faithful servant out of me. I know He has a plan for you too.

CHAPTER 1

What Is Godkward?

This is a story about hope, renewal, recovery, humility, and surrendering control. It's a story about faith, trust, and uncertainty. It's a story about finding one's purpose and the realization that perhaps we are not meant to understand that purpose until God has finished preparing us for greatness. Spoiler alert! Jesus tells us our purpose in the book of John.

> *Jesus told them,* This is the only work God wants from you: Believe in the one He has sent. *(John 6:29, NLT)*

Mostly, this is a book about God moments in my life. It's about those times in your life when you recognize God's presence, guidance, and blessings and, maybe more importantly, about when you don't. My story is an example of how God can use anyone—even a binge drinker who enjoyed partying too much—to advance His Kingdom.

As strange as it sounds, God moments started guiding me when I was furthest from Him. I had grown up in a Christian family. My grandfather pastored the Baptist church we attended. However, like many young adults, I was more interested in the party scene than the church scene. Then God changed my life with a blast of reality that started with a three-day bender and resulted in criminal charges and a life-altering ultimatum from my wife.

I never expected God would lead me on a journey that led from underage drinking at college to Alcoholics Anonymous (AA) meetings just to revive and strengthen my relationship with Him. I'm sure I'm not unique in drinking beer in college. I'm even certain I'm not the only thirty something who has had a rough night after drinking. However, it took me a long time to figure out how to turn off those college binge-drinking habits. I couldn't stop. My partying got worse as my responsibilities grew. Fortunately, God intervened before alcohol took over my life. In fact, I'd say the first AA meeting I attended was the first of many God-given, awkward moments—affectionately referred to in the rest of the book as *Godkward*.

A Godkward moment is an almost unnatural awareness of a situation where you have the option to choose a direction: to be obedient and do God's work or to look the other way and pretend like it never happened. It's a struggle to decide whether to be brave in a Godkward moment or to protect one's comfort level and social appearance before others. This book will showcase some of those Godkward moments that have helped lead me away from pain and into recovery. You can't find Godkward in the dictionary, so I define it as the presence of God amid a difficult or hard to deal with situation. Perhaps it is even a situation that causes embarrassment and inconvenience best navigated with the guidance of the Holy Spirit. It is an openness and sensitivity to what God is doing.

Maybe it's accepting a friend's invitation to go to church or inviting a friend to church. Perhaps it's telling someone you'll pray for them—and then actually doing it! Perhaps it's praying with them. Maybe it's as simple as saying "hello" to a stranger, giving money to a panhandler, or giving up your spot in the checkout line to someone else. We've been created to serve; He's called us all for a greater purpose. Godkwardness starts by listening to a higher power, rather than following your own natural instinct. To understand how Godkward moments led me out of my comfort zone and into serving Him, you first must understand how He woke me up with the events that led to a pivotal time in my life. These moments have transformed me, my thoughts, and my actions.

CHAPTER 2

Rock Bottom

I took my last drink on July 23, 2016. I had never been a daily drinker, but when I drank, I drank hard. This had been going on since my early college days, when my responsibilities were minimal. Now, with a wife, a three-year-old daughter, and a baby on the way, I started thinking of excuses to party as an escape. The sequence of events that led to my sobriety started about three months before I quit.

My wife, Lindsey, and I got the news that her father had been diagnosed with terminal cancer. My wife, who was a few months pregnant and already emotional at the time, took the news extremely hard. I was saddened by the news and knew it was my job to comfort her. My in-laws lived in Youngstown, Ohio, about two-and-a-half hours from where we live outside Columbus. A few weeks later, we still had not had a chance to go visit him, and Lindsey had internal images of her father withering away from the cancer. I knew more rationally that was probably not the case. However, if I could get her to go visit him, it would solve the irrationality and the intense emotional turmoil, at least in my mind. She agreed. With my daughter in tow, they went away for the weekend to visit Grandpa. I stayed behind because I had to work that Saturday. At some point I realized this would be a golden opportunity to let loose and have a bachelor weekend. As sick as it sounds, the devil had control of my thoughts and actions and tempted me with a weekend of partying and drinking. I wanted my wife to get to talk to her dad in person so maybe she would worry less about him. I convinced myself my motives were pure; however, I also thought I'd get to live every father's dream. At some point every dad wishes he could go back in time to escape the demands and monotony of parenthood and family— and I had the perfect excuse.

When they left town, it was time to uncage the lion. I got some coworkers together for a round of golf. During the round, I consumed twelve Miller Lites. Afterward, we lounged on the patio, where I indulged in two double shots of vodka and Gatorade.

After all, I had to rehydrate myself on a hot July afternoon.

We wrapped things up at the course around 4:00 p.m. One of my buddies and I decided it would be a shame to shut things down so early. We headed over to a local pub for dinner. To illustrate how drunk I already was, we got kicked out before we even had our drink orders taken. Luckily for us, there was a bar next door where we could quench our thirst.

That is where my memories of the evening end. I can only tell you the rest based on what my buddy helped me piece together. Several hours and drinks later, I apparently refused a ride home from his sober wife. I proceeded to get behind the wheel of my own car and somehow managed to drive 20 minutes home in one piece. I do not remember arriving.

My next memory is waking up shivering on the couch in my basement. I was still quite drunk when I walked up the stairs to a less-than-pleased wife, who was kind enough to show me pictures of how she and my daughter found me when they got home from visiting her father. The pictures revealed me passed out in a pile of my own vomit in our sunroom. She sarcastically wished me a happy anniversary. Yes, this was Monday, July 18, 2016, our seventh wedding anniversary. Lucky her.

No big deal, though, right? I'd been in that dog house before. I had an incredible 3-day golf tournament coming up later in the week, and I knew exactly what to say to get my wife to cool down. "I overdid it. The heat got to me. It will *never* happen again!"

Three days later, my wife was still upset at me, but I had made a commitment to a relative on her side of the family to play in the golf tournament. I knew keeping that commitment, to a guy I hadn't seen since my wedding, meant breaking the one I had just made to my wife about never drinking again. It was a lackluster commitment made in an effort to appease my spouse so I could continue my drinking without feeling the guilt of her disdain. So Lindsey and I agreed that it was best if I didn't come home until the tournament was over since we both knew I would be hitting the alcohol pretty hard again all weekend.

I think it is important to take a minute and inject a thought about how protective I was about my drinking. I had gotten so good at excusing my drunken behavior. Even my spouse had no choice but to abandon hope of me quitting and settle for promises that I only drink in her absence. This suited me. I was excused. It wasn't fun having a spouse eye-balling me with every drink anyway. This worked better. My love affair with partying was no longer a secret. I could golf, drink, and stay out all night, but I just couldn't come home. Sold.

We drinkers have a funny mind-set about the way we cover our tracks after a drunken escapade. Isn't it weird that as a society we can chalk up idiotic meltdowns, poor decision-making, aggressive behavior, and brutal honesty with a simple phrase "Sorry, I was drunk"? Jamie Foxx even wrote a catchy song about it: Hey, "Blame it on the goose, gotcha feeling loose, blame it on the 'tron, got ya in the zone, blame it on the al-al-alcohol." With this in mind, I often found myself making excuses for why I was so wasted: "Somebody drugged me! I didn't eat anything all day! I just need to stick to beer! Beer before liquor, never been sicker! I mixed too many types of alcohol." You name it, I said it. I even believed it. Can anyone relate?

Let's review that golf tournament with a narrative.

Day 1

When the tournament began, so did the drinking. I started drinking beer when we teed off at 9:30 a.m., and I hardly remember the round. I wasn't thrilled with the company of my distant relative. I didn't know him well, so drinking would help me be more at ease. Plus, I had a three-day hall pass that was not going to go to waste.

That night, I invited a friend to join me at the course's pub for drinks. He was going to give me a place to crash that weekend. We soon left and wound up at a strip club. I knew my wife hated those places, but I was under the influence, so who cared? We didn't get back to my friend's house until three the next morning.

We decided to stay up and drink some more and ended up in a pretty bad argument. I don't even remember what it was about, but I have heard I can be quite annoying when I've been drinking, so I'm certain I was the antagonizer. I had worn out my welcome on the first night. He kicked me out around 6:00 a.m. Since I couldn't go home, I decided to Uber back to the course. Sleep was out of the question since I would never be able to wake up for the tee time. So I hit the showers in the locker room to reinvigorate myself. Job well done.

Day 2

The second day of the tournament started with my relative telling me how impressed he was that I made it through the night with no sleep. Like any good drinker, I would have to up my game if I were going to weather the storm of an all-night rager. Before long, I had an ice-cold Jack and Coke to put a little hair of the dog back into my system. After a few of those, I had the courage to get back into the beer. Again, I don't remember anything about playing golf except that I was starting to bother my relative, who actually had a chance to win the tournament.

That night I got to know some of the other golfers in the tournament at the bar. I was notorious for leaving the group I had come to the bar with to meet new people. I knew no strangers. I was the life of the party—anyone's party! One of the guys I had been talking to said he was having a party back at his place and invited me to tag along. He had a pool, which was clutch. I had been awake and drinking for thirty-six hours at that point and needed a way to revitalize. We drank and swam until 4:00 a.m., when the other guys decided it was time to shut the party down.

I knew once again that if I fell asleep at that point, I wouldn't be able to honor my commitment to golf in a few short hours. I asked if I could take a beer for the road and somehow found my way back to the course's parking lot. I tried to get into the locker room for a repeat of the previous morning, but it was locked. Apparently the course isn't open at 4:30 a.m.

I remember getting into my car and deciding to wait. I must have blacked out, though, because I woke up shivering in the locker room under a pile of towels. I was clueless about how I got there or why I was so cold.

When my relative saw me, he was embarrassed and furious! I tried to jokingly ask what happened. He told me that when the course employees arrived for the day, they found me passed out on a putting green getting soaked by sprinklers. They nearly called an ambulance because I was unresponsive. He told me that the head pro of the course was also pretty upset, so I went directly to him to make amends. "Hey, at least I didn't drive anywhere," I joked with him. I was always great at rebounding, manipulating one's impression of my drinking, at least in my mind.

Day 3

By the third day, I had been unconscious for maybe three hours of the last forty-eight and had consumed too many drinks to count. There was only one way to rally: fill it up again! I was planning to start slow, but when I asked the bartender for a Jack and Coke, the lid fell off the bottle while she was pouring. "The extra-strong drink was fine by me," I told her. In fact, maybe it was a good thing.

Needless to say, I don't remember a single hole, or even a single stroke, of golf that day either. I do remember feeling like a legend out there, though. Word of my shenanigans the night before had spread. Perfect strangers were coming up asking me if I was "that guy" and praising me for my resilience. It's interesting that no one was willing or ready to really confront me or the real problem at hand.

After golf, we drank and partied even more. Around 10:00 p.m., my relative came looking for me, red hot because I had been putting drinks on his tab all day. Ironically, the guy who had invited me was getting on my nerves—what a flawed sense of perception. I wanted him to know that I deserved to be there more than him—that people liked me more than him. I called the bartender over right away and overpaid on the tab just to undermine him. Then I asked the bartender to tell him to pipe down, which made him even angrier. He got in my face, and by God's grace, I didn't react. Perhaps I couldn't muster the energy to stand up to him, so amazingly I walked away. He was so irate they kicked him out of the bar. On his way out, he shouted that he would be calling my wife to tell her all of my shenanigans I'd managed to keep a secret until now.

I thought he was bluffing, so I didn't really care at the time. Then, around 11:30 p.m., the other shoe dropped, and I got a text from my wife telling me not to bother coming home. Now that hit a nerve with me. I didn't think any of this mess was my fault, and I blamed my relative. What happened to the "Bro Code"? So I texted and then ended up calling him to give him an ugly piece of my mind. The voice message I left him resulted in a suspended thirty-day jail sentence pending I complete counseling and twelve months of probation. That was a major dose of reality. Imagine how far down I had fallen. What was to be a fun, stress-relieving weekend had resulted in poor decisions and challenging circumstances.

The Ultimatum

After much begging and pleading the next day, my wife graciously let me come home, albeit to present me with an ultimatum. "Drink again and I'm taking the kids and leaving," she said.

Sure, sure, I thought. *I've heard this one before. This too shall pass.*

I had literally turned that mentality of hers around six days ago. I wasn't worried that she would leave until I received another phone call. My mother-in-law had been involved in some of my drunken escapades before. She was tired of seeing her daughter get hurt and told me, "If you ever hurt her again, I will utilize every resource I have to get her out of the marriage." There was real hatred and genuine spite in her words to me. She was ready to defend her baby and grandbabies. I felt the heat, so I complied. I agreed to get help and go to AA to avoid losing my family.

Thinking back on this now, I see how God had his fingertip on everything that was going on in my life. I'd heard similar ultimatums and reacted differently. I also think I would have shrugged this one off if I had still been living in Cleveland, where I grew up and had family and friends. I think I could have even rationalized single parenting if I'd been closer to that support network. I would have also had places to stay if I got kicked out. Being so far away made those consequences to drinking again seem impossible. Up there I had a crew; down here I felt stranded. God knew what he was doing moving us to Columbus. He would change my life and knew best how to reach me.

CHAPTER 3

My AA Experience

Alcoholics Anonymous—these words carry quite the reputation. Let's take a minute and address the elephant in the room for those who haven't attended an AA meeting. I'll admit before I attended I thought of AA as a weird cult made up of criminals and homeless vagabonds who liked drinking diesel coffee and smoking three packs of cigarettes a day. I'd imagine I'm not the only one who has that image, so I want to provide some context as to what an AA meeting looks and feels like. There are different styles of meetings. Some have guest speakers that share their story of sobriety with the group and are the main speaker. Others, like the one I attend regularly, are an open forum. It's a group of folks like you and me that have struggled making wise decisions with alcohol. The ages I've seen are anywhere from twenty-one to eighty-one. I've seen day-one beginners, and I've seen those that have attended meetings for three decades religiously. The rooms are filled with successful entrepreneurs and executives, managers and sales representatives, stay-at-home parents, and college students. Some in attendance are court ordered and some spousal ordered. Some attendees have family in the picture still, and some have burned every bridge. There are those who drive fancy cars and those who need a ride home. Some attend one meeting a week, and others attend three a day. I would imagine if you were to go into any restaurant on any Friday or Saturday night and did an anonymous survey, you'd find a number of individuals who either have been to an AA meeting themselves or have family members who have. Addiction does not discriminate by race, religion, color, or creed. No one is immune to the reach of alcohol and its impact on relationships.

Since I began sharing my story, you'd be surprised how many people have said things to me like "I think I may have a problem," but then I'm like, "Nah, I'm good," or "I am not sure how to deal with my boyfriend/girlfriend or spouse because they have a problem." The way I see it, everyone who drinks has a problem of some sort. As a matter of fact, that's most often what causes us to drink. I've had and heard about problems, such as "I'm antisocial, but I'm at a party. Gulp! I'm stressed out from work and need to relax. Gulp! Everyone else is drinking and I need to fit in. Gulp!" Drinking always starts with a problem, and soon it can become the problem.

On my way to my first meeting, I couldn't believe what I was doing. How could I possibly be at this point? I was so overwhelmed by nerves I almost pulled over to kill an hour in a parking lot instead of going to the meeting. My wife never would have known. She had no idea what a meeting would be like either. I could just make something up when I got home and let the lies continue. After all, I didn't belong with AA people, did I? I didn't feel like an alcoholic. I still don't think I was ever chemically dependent on alcohol. I was never a daily drinker. I never needed it. I just liked the party scene and tended to go a little overboard. It was easy to make excuses and rationalize my behavior.

I kept driving. God gave me an extreme amount of courage to get out of my car and go into that first meeting. The only person I had spoken to who had experience with AA was my brother. He assured me it wasn't a big deal. He told me to just go sit for an hour and it would be over. It was advice from someone who had also been mandated to go. I would try to get in and out of there saying and doing as little as possible.

God had other plans.

"Welcome," said the gentleman who seemed to be leading the meeting as I walked in the door. I returned the greeting and found a seat. A minute later he approached me and asked if I'd "read the promises" in front of the group.

"This is my first meeting," I said.

"That's okay," he assured me. "It's just like any other meeting."

"Oh, I'm sorry," I said. "I mean, like, this is my first ever AA meeting."

"Oh, I'm so sorry," he said, caught off guard. "Don't worry about it. I'm glad you're here."

That was one of those Godkward moments where God pushed me out of my comfort zone to take a step of faith. It may seem small, but to me it was a huge deal. Because I'd taken the steps to attend the meeting, I told myself and the gentleman, "I'll do it." Of course, he told me I didn't have to, but I thought since I'd come this far I might as well read the thing.

Moments after the 7:00 p.m. start time, he called my name to come up and read a laminated copy of the Promises of AA. I looked into the crowd, said "hello," and then clumsily said "Oh, and I guess I'm an alcoholic." There were probably twenty people in the room, and a few sentences in, I choked up. I mean I cried. I knew as I read that paper that I wanted to be freed from the grips of this continual pain. The AA paperwork I was reading promised to do so if I followed the steps. It was through this Godkward moment that I bought into this process.

CHAPTER 4

Sober Living

Life without drinking wasn't too difficult on a day-to-day basis. The weekends might not even be that bad now that I had made a commitment not to party. The temptation to drink would be strongest during activities I usually did with a beer in my hand. As summer stretched into fall, I began to worry about one thing specifically: football.

In Columbus, Ohio, Buckeyes football was king. Saturdays in the fall would become my biggest challenge yet. For alcoholics it can be easy to rationalize having "just a couple" in moments of temptation. I knew "just a couple" meant a flood of problems. I prayed for God to give me strength and wisdom. I would need it to navigate my challenges.

The answer to my prayers came when God nudged me toward my next Godkward moment. I had been attending Adventure Church for a couple of months now. I was beginning to grow spiritually and I was genuinely enjoying the fellowship. One Sunday, Pastor Kyle Hammond announced that the church was looking for more people to be life group leaders. The purpose of life groups at Adventure Church was to get people out of rows and into circles. In other words, it was to form smaller groups of believers to get to know each other better and form a community. Most of these groups were based on the weekly sermon or followed a Bible study. I didn't know if I was ready for that yet. Fortunately, I didn't have to be. Kyle said the groups were meant for Christians to "do life together," and they could be about anything.

"Anything?" I asked when I saw him out in the lobby. The spirit had planted a seed in my mind during the service.

"What do you have in mind?" he asked.

"Buckeyes football," I said, expecting him to ask for my rationale. Instead, he gave me the go-ahead.

My motive and primary purpose for the group was to find a way to enjoy watching football without alcohol. If I started the group, then I'd have some church guys to come over and watch football within a safe environment.

I had it made, now. I was even fighting less with my wife. When I had been drinking, I never liked it when she stayed mad at me for longer than ten minutes after I apologized for my drunken behavior. However, after a whole month of sobriety, she still hadn't forgiven me for all the times I'd embarrassed her over the years. She hadn't forgiven me for hurting her emotionally. She shared her feelings with me: loneliness, inadequacy, low self-esteem, rejection, never being good enough, and, more than anything, anxiety. I caused all these feelings over the years in one way or another. For example, I'd always choose going out and drinking over staying in to watch a movie with her. I'd always tell her she was the problem and that if I were going to be condemned for getting drunk before I even had a drink, I might as well see it through. I had embarrassed her countless times in front of other people with my drunken behavior. I've wrecked vacations with both sides of our family. I've even made a fool out of myself in front of strangers for a good laugh. Who would want to be married to the guy who goes streaking through the party or vomits and pees all over a friend's guest room while staying the night? Oh yes, these are real stories and clearly not my brightest moments.

After not being forgiven a month into sobriety, I felt that she needed a relationship with God and a Christian community too. Her closest friend moved out of town months before, so she didn't have anyone to talk to about her emotions. At least, that was my diagnosis. So my objective for starting a life group became twofold: one, to learn how to hang out and watch football with guys and not feel pressured to drink and, two, to get close enough with these guys so we could get our families together. Then, hopefully, my wife would enjoy hanging out with their wives.

Since I'm being completely honest here, though, I have to come clean that I had another motive for starting a life group: I was certain nobody would join. I knew it would be an easy way out. As usual, though, God had different plans. What I thought I knew wasn't in His grand design.

Our first life group meeting was on September 17, 2016, to watch the Buckeyes take on the Oklahoma Sooners. Three other guys showed up. One was a good friend (who drank), one was an acquaintance, and the other was a guy I had only met at church once and invited to join the group.

Between the guys I didn't know too well and the fact that I'd never done anything like this before, I was already feeling rather uncomfortable. On top of that, severe weather in Oklahoma delayed the game a good two hours. The guys showed up on time, so this was definitely becoming awkward. God showed up though, as He promises in the Bible.

> *For where two or three gather together as my followers, I am there among them. (Matthew 18:20, NLT)*

God turned it into Godkward, and we ended up having a great night. Since the game didn't start on time, we were forced to talk and get to know each other. By kickoff, I was much more relaxed. Even though the game didn't end until well after midnight, I saw them all at church the next morning, and they even wanted to do it again. We continued to meet about every other week for the duration of the college football season.

The last week of the season, or Michigan week, was the biggest game of the year. We decided to get the families together. The kids played, the wives talked, and the Buckeyes won, clinching a spot in the College Football Playoff. Since that meant they would play on New Year's Eve, we decided to have a party with the group. Even the Buckeyes' miserable loss to Clemson that night couldn't put a damper on how happy I was with the fellowship between families.

My wife and I were home and in bed by 12:01 a.m. I had successfully made it through the college football season sober. I even made some good friends in the process. A year earlier I never would have believed someone who told me that I would watch every Buckeyes' game and get through New Year's Eve without a drink in my hand. It's funny, but telling that while in the midst of the season should you have asked me how the group was going, I would have given you a comment like "Eh, all we do is watch football." After the season ended, however, I realized I had accomplished some serious goals. Look at what God did with just a little bit of faith!

CHAPTER 5

Fasting

New Year's Day fell on a Sunday, and I was convinced I was starting the new year right by getting up and going to church. After all, I'd been sober for more than five months and hadn't had a drink in 2017! During the service, Pastor Kyle previewed the next series at Adventure Church, called *Noise*. We were going to learn about and participate in a fast. I'd never participated in one before, but the concept intrigued me.

"What could I possibly give up?" I asked myself. I had already quit drinking, but I had another nasty habit—the nastiest habit: smoking. I absolutely hated that I smoked, but I've never been able to quit. I started when I was twenty and working as a server at a restaurant. I noticed the smokers were getting cigarette breaks, but nonsmokers never got fresh air breaks! I thought that was an injustice, so I picked up the habit, and the rest was history. Now it's my lungs that are screaming about injustice.

I'd tried to quit many times, even very recently. I had never tried to quit cold turkey or as part of a fast, however. So that's what I decided to do. I would quit, and when a craving came, I would ask God to remove it and pray that I needed Him more than nicotine. Could this really work for me?

The next week in church, the *Noise* series began. Fasts would start the very next day. Pastor Kyle preached about how the way to reach our desired outcome in life was not to sit back and desire. If we truly wanted results, he said, we needed to change our daily disciplines. This was what I'd done during the fast. He told us that when we experience change, there will be an associated loss. That loss comes with pain. I related this to a physical workout. For example, I could desire to lose twenty pounds as much as I wanted. For me to really lose the weight, I may have to wake up early every day (changing a daily discipline), in doing so I'd lose an hour of sleep (associated loss) and because of that I would experience a slight case of exhaustion (pain).

I'd heard about people fasting before many times. I'd even mocked it when it came to Catholics and their Friday fish fries. I'd never tried it, but this was 2017—a new year, a sober year. This was the year where I was going to begin to understand my purpose. What could it hurt to give up something for twenty-one days? I really didn't know what I was getting into. It was going to be intense.

I ultimately decided to give up cigarettes *and* pop. I have to admit that the addition wasn't as much about the extra challenge as it was a planned backup in case I couldn't actually go three weeks without smoking. On top of all that, I decided to get up an hour earlier every day so I could start my days praying and reading the word with a devotional before getting ready for work.

The devil gave me some serious doubts about getting out of bed that first morning. It was January in Ohio, and my bed was so warm, whispered Satan. What would time with God accomplish that was more important than an extra hour of sleep for my health and sanity? And who would know if I stayed in bed, anyway? I knew the devil was making it hard for me to wake up so I wouldn't grow closer to God. I took that as a positive sign and started praying: "God, I'm here. I don't want to be here, but I'm here.

Quiet my thoughts. Quiet my mind. Open up my eyes and ears so I may see and hear what you want from me today."

I started my prayers like that every morning. It's funny that we think we can hide our real thoughts from God. He knows if you're all in or not. I believe that God appreciates effort, but He appreciates honesty more. When I started being honest with Him about my feelings (which He already knew), He started to entrust me with greater responsibilities and visions. This is when I realized how rewarding it is to work for someone who already knows the outcome. It's quite liberating to give Him all of your thoughts, cares, concerns, and worries knowing He is in charge. All of that in exchange for a little bit of my mornings seemed like a good bargain!

The book I chose to read in the morning was *The One Year Uncommon Life Daily Challenge*, by Tony Dungy. My dad gave it to me a couple Christmases ago since I'm a sports fan. I'd read some sporadically in the years since receiving it, but never regularly. The first day's reading was titled "Nothing Means Nothing" and could be summed up as a reminder that nothing will ever separate us from God's love. What a great affirmation it is from God that it was worth resisting the devil's temptation to stay in bed. What I got up to do means something and is helping me grow closer to God. I ended that first morning with a prayer of thanks and asked for assistance making it through the day without becoming irritable from the withdrawal of nicotine.

I stayed strong the first couple of days and was learning to go to God as a trusted friend when I had cravings or struggled with my emotions. I was making progress. I was trying to be the best Christian version of myself and then *bam*—the stomach flu. My tone with God went from friendly to angry. "Thank you, God! Thanks so much! Are you kidding me? I am here trying not to stress out and you gave me the flu? Not just the flu, but the worst illness I've had in a decade! Real cool, God."

The next day I was still upset. I reluctantly read my devotional anyway. After all, I couldn't go to work after "the Great Purge of 2017." That day's devotion included James 1:23–24.

> *For if you listen to the word and don't obey, it is like glancing at your face in a mirror. You see yourself, walk away, and forget what you look like. (James 1:23–24, NLT)*

I wasn't quite sure what God wanted me to get from this, but I reflected anyway. While I reflected, I could still feel how sore my body was from the purge. It reminded me of a guy I'd heard about in the Bible named Job. I decided to put down my book, pick up the Bible, and read the book of Job. Something caught my eye that I'd never noticed in the story before: The devil had to ask God's permission to take things from Job, in the sense of "Sure, God, Job serves you now, but look at how well he has it. I bet if you take that stuff away, he will forget you."

I envision God replying, "Go ahead, Satan, but he's with me." The devil did everything but kill him, and Job still praised God. Finally, God told the devil to leave him alone and go fly a kite because He had a purpose for Job and ultimately restored him.

Then I realized what the Holy Spirit was trying to get me to understand: I had been mad at the wrong guy. We tend to forget that even though God is number one in the power rankings, the devil is just as real and at number two. The devil knows what we want and desires nothing but to give us what we think we need to destroy our path. I nearly started crying as I thought about how a conversation may have sounded between the devil and God about my life.

"Sure, God, Adam has it all together," I imagine the devil saying. "He grew up in church. He has his friends and family nearby. Let him go to college on his own. Okay, now put a beer in his hand. Let him experience how fun it can be to be the life of the party." Job's experience confirmed for me that I have a real enemy.

I revisit myself falling from God's grace. I went from being the boy who would sing the hymn "This Is My Father's World" in church to the twenty something crooning Billy Joel's "Piano Man" after several drinks in a karaoke bar. I went from leading a prayer in my college dorm room on September 11, 2001, to bonging beers and chasing it with tequila, hot sauce, and pickle juice later that year. I turned from being the potentially loaded early high school graduate to the undisciplined early college dropout—the avid golfer, but the more avid drinker; the guy who was fun to drink with, until he wasn't; the husband that tried to be good, but who was holding onto a single guy's party life; a father who wanted recognition for his family contributions, but was never around to receive the accolades; and a sinner saved by grace. I was one more drink from losing it all. But then God stepped in.

"Enough, Satan. Leave him alone! He's still one of mine. I have a great plan and a wonderful purpose for him," God responded. "I will restore him so he can share his story and help lead others to Me. Now go away. Let him be."

I still get goose bumps when I think about that morning. I set aside my anger about the flu and was reenergized to figure out His purpose for my life.

It took a few more days for me to recover, and by the time I felt human again, I had made it through the first challenging week of the fast. I hadn't made any progress in figuring out my purpose, though. During church on Sunday, I made up my mind that I would approach the pastor after the service and tell him I wanted to do more. That would help me figure out what areas of service I was passionate about and provide clarity about my purpose. By the end of the service, however, I lost courage and convinced myself it was just a spiritual high. The pastors are busy enough with all sorts of people coming up to them on Sundays and don't need me in the mix. Besides, if God really needed me, He would just lay it on the pastor's heart to reach out to me.

I know that's not the right way to think, but in my case it worked out. Two days later, I got an email from an associate pastor that read, "Hi, Adam. I'm wondering if you would be willing to shoot a video for viewing purposes at our services in the coming weeks to discuss what it was like to lead your first life group." Are you kidding me? My reply was an enthusiastic *Yes!*

The next day, I attended my "home" AA meeting. I'd been in the group for about five months at that point. My sponsor wanted to meet with me before the meeting to discuss the next step of the program. I'm not entirely certain which step we were working on. It's really inconsequential. However, if you've ever been curious as to what the twelve steps of recovery in the AA program are, I have listed them:

> *Step 1: We admitted we were powerless over alcohol—that our lives had become unmanageable.*
> *Step 2: We came to believe that a power greater than ourselves could restore us to sanity.*
> *Step 3: We made a decision to turn our will and our lives over to the care of God as we understood Him.*
> *Step 4: We made a searching and fearless moral inventory of ourselves.*

Step 5: We admitted to God, to ourselves, and to another human being the exact nature of our wrongs.

Step 6: We were entirely ready to have God remove all these defects of character.

Step 7: We humbly asked Him to remove our shortcomings.

Step 8: We made a list of all persons we had harmed and became willing to make amends to them all.

Step 9: We made direct amends to such people wherever possible, except when to do so would injure them or others.

Step 10: We continued to take personal inventory and when we were wrong promptly admitted it.

Step 11: We sought through prayer and meditation to improve our conscious contact with God, as we understood Him, praying only for knowledge of His will for us and the power to carry that out.

Step 12: Having had a spiritual awakening as the result of these steps, we tried to carry this message to alcoholics and to practice these principles in all our affairs.

I told my sponsor about my fast and how it had made me closer to God. He was impressed. I was so fired up that I told him I would share about what God is doing in my life if the topic was raised that night.

Later on during the meeting, the AA secretary asks, "Are there any burning desire topics anyone would care to address tonight?"

Silence—deafening silence for maybe two to three minutes. No one spoke.

Finally, an older gentleman started to speak trying to hold back tears. "I'd like some experience, strength and hope from someone about what your Higher Power has done for you."

AA has God's fingerprints all over it. God is referenced all throughout the steps and throughout the *AA Big Book*. However, in an effort to create a program that is welcoming to all walks of life, they leave the definition of God up to each individual: God as one understands Him. This could be anything from God the Father, Son, and Holy Spirit to a positive energy force in the universe and to mother nature. Anything goes. And as long as it helps keep you sober, it's doing its part as far as AA is concerned. I'm not here to change the steps or to condemn those with different beliefs; I just want to encourage anyone reading this who feels like they couldn't do AA because they aren't religious to rethink that. This organization and its mission has helped many in their journey into recovery.

After the gentleman brought up the topic of a higher power, I almost burst out laughing because it was such a Godkward moment. I looked at my sponsor and said, "I guess that's my queue!" I began to share my story focusing on the request that had been made. I could have talked all night, but with respect for other's time, I decided to hit on the four most important things going on in my life at the time. First, God has kept me alive. If I were dead, I couldn't serve His purpose. I'm certain He has kept me out of harm's way when my drinking led me to make dangerous decisions numerous times. Second, He made me relatable. It sounds juvenile, but when someone with authority tells us what to do and what not to do, we tend to think they don't understand. My testimony is one of weakness. I'm not perfect. I have little to give. It's God who is making use of my little and multiplying it in a way I never would have dreamed. Third, He gave me courage to speak to a crowd of strangers—courage used to be something I got from drinking. Now I get it from knowing who gives me direction. Finally, He gave me the curiosity to continue to pursue my purpose. Had it not been for this curiosity, I would have been reluctant to take any next steps. I would have hesitated because I wouldn't know if it was the correct next step. So often I'm conflicted about which way I should go. You might say I have been paralyzed by uncertainty at times, but my curiosity to see what happens next drove me to pursue God's purpose for my life. What that may be, I did not yet know.

Brief silence and uneasy shuffling filled the room as my voice trailed off. I think what I said was received well, but in AA we don't talk to anyone directly. It's an open forum to state your thoughts and not direct them at anyone in particular. This is challenging for me sometimes, but God reminds me it is not my job to understand how someone receives my message. My job is to deliver the message. He will set the hearts of those listening.

Not knowing my purpose was a sticking point with me as I left the meeting. If I am going to be successful in finding my purpose, it will have to start at home. When I got into bed that night, I prayed for guidance in being a leader God would be proud of with my family.

The next morning my alarm went off at five thirty. I hopped out of bed, but my wife was not in the room. I found her in the kitchen, decidedly awake from the two-month-old baby boy whom we let stay down the hall. I thought about my prayer from the night before and seized the opportunity. I asked my wife, "Do you want to see what I get up to do so early in the morning?"

The next thing I know, she said yes. I gulped because I'm about to lead her in a devotion for the first time. It felt weird. We had been married for almost eight years. We were lovers and fighters, but never prayers. But didn't I just ask for this opportunity a mere eight hours before?

I started by praying aloud for God to open our hearts and clear our minds and the desire to focus solely on Him. I opened the devotion book and turned to that day's reading titled "True Civil Disobedience." I hesitantly read aloud because I was not sure what it will say or if it's the best topic for our first couples' devotion. I asked for her opinion when I was done reading, and she said, "I don't think that was a good one for me to start with." Admittedly, it didn't hit me at all either, so I decided to open up the Bible to the scripture verses from the reading. Hopefully, that will provide further instruction and insight. First, we opened to Romans 13:1, where Paul tells the Christians in Rome to submit to governing authority because there is no authority except which God has established. This was a day before the inauguration of the most controversial president-elect in modern history. Not wanting to bring up politics at the time, I quickly moved on to find a battle cry that seemed to match exactly where I was at in my walk with God.

> *And do this, understanding the present time: The hour has already come for you to wake up from your slumber, because our salvation is nearer now than when we first believed. The night is nearly over: the day is almost here. So let us put aside the deeds of darkness and put on the armor of light. (Romans 13:11–12, NIV)*

God was telling me to wake up! He is coming back one day.

"Now is the time to prepare, Adam!" I heard the Holy Spirit saying. "Here is your purpose: Change your ways, use your platform, and lead people to me!"

Who, me? I thought. *Lead people to you? How? All I did was ask my wife to do a devotional and pray with me. And now I'm supposed to be a leader? I guess we're done with baby steps!*

Later that day, my wife, a dentist, asked me to talk with her about a potential job opportunity. It required some sensitive decision-making. She had been offered the opportunity to partner up to purchase her own dental practice. Life was hectic with two small children. Job security, maybe more so income security, was the real stress point for us at the time. We both want her to own a practice one day, but is that day today? I told her we should pray about it and get some more facts and then we can make our decision.

The next morning, I woke up at the first ding of the alarm. I was so excited, focused, and eager to hear from God. The scripture I studied from my devotion was 1 Corinthians 11. I found the passage and was stunned by what I saw. My study Bible had a text box about an inch below the chapter entitled "Making choices on sensitive issues." I was speechless. I caught my wife on my way upstairs to get ready for work and said with a chuckle, "I'm pretty sure this one was meant for you." I laid it on the table and asked her to read and use it when she made a decision about the job. It listed nine items Christ himself wants us to weigh before making a choice, all supported by scripture. I said a prayer of thanks as I got ready for the rest of my day. God knew where we were and what we were dealing with.

I was still fired up about how God was moving in my life when I got to work. Shortly after, I fired up my computer, and I got an email from a woman I've never met. She told me she got my email on the church web site along with the information about my life group for men. She asked if I'd reach out to her shy son. She told me he was new to the church and wanted to get plugged in but wasn't sure how. I assured her that I'll reach out right away. I had decided to expand my football group when the season was over and was hoping more men would join. I was blown away by another Godkward moment! I emailed her son and got a response later in the day saying, "Thank you so much for reaching out. I would love to see what your group is all about. Just let me know where and when." God was confirming for me that I was taking the right steps. And aside from the sickness I had earlier in the fast, things had been smooth sailing. But to paraphrase Allen Iverson, "We talkin' about practice, man!" God was laying a foundation. He was training me—preparing me. Little did I know I would soon go through the most traumatizing event of my life as a father.

CHAPTER 6

Toddler of God

Seven months of sobriety.

A successful fast.

A growing men's life group.

A growing family with the addition of a baby boy.

My priorities were straight, my faith was in action, and I was working toward God's purpose in my life.

That's when the enemy took notice and began testing my faith again. Satan knows when he is losing us. He hates to see us succeed. All of the things God wants for us, the devil wishes for us to blunder. And wouldn't you know it? Just when things were going my way, just like the enemy has done in the past, he threw a curveball my way.

My three-month-old son, Grady, had to be taken to the emergency room. This was following an ER visit exactly two weeks earlier (bad cold and double ear infection), an urgent care trip two nights earlier (bronchiolitis), and an appointment with his regular pediatrician the morning before. None of these doctors could have prevented what he was about to go through this time. Grady had respiratory syncytial virus, commonly known as RSV. It had been running rampant among little children that year, and he would not be immune to the challenges it would bring.

As his father, I thought he'd get better with some meds, maybe a few shots, a couple of hugs, and a kiss. Little did I know how detrimental RSV could be to tiny lungs. For most babies and young children, the RSV infection causes nothing more than a cold. But for a small percentage, infection with RSV can lead to serious problems such as bronchiolitis, which is inflammation of the small airways of the lungs, or pneumonia, which can become life-threatening. I would soon feel like I was living a nightmare. How could this be happening to my family?

The first day we were there, I couldn't believe it when Grady was admitted to the Pediatric Intensive Care Unit (PICU). I rationalized it as the doctors just being overly cautious. Shortly after we got there, however, a doctor entered the room and said, "Mom and Dad, you may want to sit down." That is not a phrase any parent wants to hear in a hospital. The doctor told us Grady was in for the long haul. We'd have to ride out the storm because they couldn't treat the illness, just the symptoms. What brought us here would keep us here. At least we felt we were in good hands.

Thinking back, we were so blessed to have such wonderful, enthusiastic caregivers at Nationwide Children's Hospital. At the time, however, we were so exhausted, especially my wife. She had stayed up with him the entire night before (as mothers do). As the man of the family, I thought my job was to show that even in the roughest storms, dads don't get sick. Yea right! Ducks on a pond, that's what dads are like. On the surface, we seem calm; but under the water, we are paddling for our lives, uncertain, insecure, and troubled that we can't solve the problem.

I was taking in so much information about Grady's condition and trying not to get overwhelmed. I learned all about RSV. I learned what a CPT, BiPAP mask, and an arterial blood gas were. I felt like I was halfway to a medical terminology degree (no offense to anyone actually in that profession).

More importantly, I was learning more about my faith. The Bible says we are to have the faith of a child. I was about to learn the truth in the phrases "God the Father" and "Child of God." I was, and still am, a toddler of God. No, really. I'm demanding and disobedient; I toe the line every chance I get. I want my way, yet rarely heed His warnings.

I find God will often treat me like a toddler too. If I listen, He will continue to speak. If I stray, He will try to get my attention. If I follow His directions, He will give me more responsibility. If I ask for something, He'll give it to me (in His time, of course). When I fall, He dusts me off. When I miss a shot, He rebounds, passes it back, and tells me to shoot again. He loves me and cares for me. Just as I want to see my children succeed, He wants to see me fulfill my purpose. He wants me to contribute. He wants me to be patient. He wants me to be selfless. He wants me to persevere. He wants me to seek Him first. In short, He wants me—all of me. I knew all of this, of course, but God put me in the PICU with Grady so I could experience Him and His power firsthand.

I hadn't left Grady's side all day and was beginning to wonder where God was as more tubes and machines were hooked up to his little body. My head was spinning. The devil was beginning to win control of my thoughts.

I stepped out of the room to clear my mind. I checked my email and had one from a religious group that I signed up for at some point. It was a marketing email, but it had a Bible verse attached:

> *Who here by worrying has added another minute to his life? (Matthew 6:37, NLT)*

Okay, there you are, God, I thought. *I knew you were here, but now I feel better. I remember you are in control. Thanks.*

The next couple of days went by in a blur. Hospitals are like casinos in that you lose all sense of time, and by the time you leave, you've lost all of your money. The same doubts were starting to creep back into my thoughts as I watched my son get skewered through every hole in his body with some sort of tube.

All of a sudden, my phone buzzed and an alert from the Bible app caught my attention. It's amazing how high tech God is becoming in communicating with us when we need Him most. It was the verse of the day:

You made all the delicate, inner parts of my body and knit me together in my mother's womb. Thank you for making me so wonderfully complex! Your workmanship is marvelous—how well I know it. (Psalm 139:13–14, NLT)

I started to have a conversation with God.

"Okeydoke, God. You're right. You got this. I know fears have been distracting me from you. I know I've been holding a false bravado in front of everyone. Hey, do you mind if I cry a bit?"

My wife had gone back to work to support our son's gambling, err hospital, habit. I was all alone except for Grady. I let my emotions come to the surface and tears drip to the floor of that hospital room. I was broken.

The next morning was the start of our fourth day in the hospital. I had only seen my daughter once since we'd been there, as she was transferred from the care of my sister-in-law to my mother. I was so tired, but I wanted to see her more than anything. She was my princess and needed to feel special too. It was time for a daddy–daughter date.

I stopped and got Mackenzie flowers on my way to pick her up from preschool. She was blown away, and I was about to spoil her even more. I treated her to her favorite restaurant: Cracker Barrel. After dinner, we headed home for some dancing and wrestling. Then daddy was off again to camp out with Bubba at the PICU.

On the way back to the hospital, I was already feeling guilty and emotional from having to say bye to Mackenzie again when a song came on the radio that absolutely chewed me up inside. So maybe it was those raw emotions or maybe my fatigue, or just maybe it was that I was hearing the lyrics to my life. The song was "Lead Me," by Sanctus Real. The chorus goes:

> *Lead me with strong hands*
> *Stand up when I can't*
> *Don't leave me hungry for love*
> *Chasing dreams, what about us?*
>
> *Show me you're willing to fight*
> *That I'm still the love of your life*
> *I know we call this our home*
> *But I still feel alone*

I felt chewed up and spit out. I wanted to do all of those things for my wife and children. But I couldn't do it alone. I was tired. I was ragged. I needed a hope and peace.

The next day I woke up to my in-laws lugging back into the room from their quick turnaround. They had been driving back and forth between Youngstown and Columbus all week to help us out. Seven short months ago, my mother-in-law helped scare me into sobriety. That morning, I brought her to tears when I shared those lyrics with her.

After they left to take care of Mackenzie, I checked the Bible verse of the day on my phone. What kind of inspiration will God provide today?

> *Wait patiently for the Lord. Be brave*
> *and courageous. Yes, wait patiently*
> *for the Lord. (Psalm 27:14, NLT)*

Ha! I love you, God! I thought. *You're my type of guy. You literally just told me to suck it up. You're on the way!*

A little while later, I knew it was God watching over us as the doctors took the tube out of Grady's throat. What a relief! Maybe we'll be on our way home soon!

"Not so fast," the doctors cautioned. "He still has a long way to go."

By that evening, however, Grady's condition had improved enough to be transferred out of the PICU. That was an answer to my prayers—a victory. So, of course, the devil had to make an appearance. With Grady seemingly on the mend and my wife and I extremely exhausted, the enemy pounced. He distracted us from the good developments with Grady's health with an unpleasant topic: finances. Did you know you can't pay a hospital bill with credit card rewards points? That's a shame. But shame on us for ruining a short window of happiness in a stress-filled week with an argument about something we couldn't control.

When my wife left later that night, I even went as far as to think "woe is me!" I'm always the one apologizing. When will I be recognized for my contributions?

I was still irritated and in a bad mood when I woke up the next morning. We'd been in the hospital almost a week. I wasn't just tired; I was wiped out, angry, and defeated. I was even upset at God because He didn't feed me anything with the verse of the day. It was 1 Corinthians 1:10, which is basically Paul talking about division among church leaders. What good does that do me? Give me something relevant in helping with my current situation, please!

My in-laws arrived and gave me a much-needed break from the hospital room. I decided I needed a good breakfast. I walked across the street to a restaurant and got seated next to three gentlemen who were being rather boisterous. Do you ever look at your phone as a cover while listening to the table next to you? Of course not. Me neither.

I split my focus between my pancakes, my phone, and their conversation. Then I overheard something interesting. They were all pastors. They were talking about their work and how other pastors were giving them a bad rap concluding that they preach to get rich—they don't do it for the right reasons. I smirked because I happened to be looking at the 1 Corinthians verse of the day to mask my eavesdropping. Then, I shook my head because I felt another Godkward moment in the works. Seriously, God. No! God wanted me to interrupt those guys and talk to them. Yea, right!

What was I supposed to say?

"Hey, I couldn't help but overhear, and uhhh, my Bible verse I was just reading says something along those lines."

I kept shooting up excuses, and God kept knocking them back down. Next thing I know, I cleared my throat and made that Godkward interruption. And I'm so glad I did. We got to talking about what brought me there that morning. Then one of the pastors asked my son's name and if we could all pray over him. We prayed out loud, right there in the restaurant. There were other people there, but we did not care what they thought. It was powerful prayer.

After we prayed, another one of the pastors began relating to my story. He had a child who went through something similar. He encouraged me by sharing about when his son was in the ER, the doctors were concerned that his oxygen saturation levels were too low. When they were about to transfer his son to the PICU, the Holy Spirit spoke and told him his son's oxygen levels were going to get to 100 before they got there. I bet you can guess what the machine said when they plugged it back in: 100! Praise God.

We shook hands as they left, and I couldn't help but smile about how God placed me in that situation. He puts you in situations every day to give you the opportunity to learn from Him. I didn't want to talk to people I didn't know, but I'm glad I did. I asked the waitress for a cup of coffee to go and got out my wallet to pay. She said "No, no. Your bill has been paid. Have a great day!"

I fought back the tears in my eyes. I had just been throwing myself a pity party feeling as if I'm the only one who goes out of the way to help someone else. God saw that. He heard me, just as He always does. He spoke to me, just as He always does. This time, I listened.

I returned to Grady's room after breakfast to the news that in the hour I was gone, the doctors were able to remove his oxygen tube. My son was breathing on his own for the first time in a week! Is it a coincidence that I had just had strangers pray for him about this exact thing? Nope! I can't calculate that statistical probability, but I can say confidently that God heard those prayers. I felt his touching hand on me in that moment. I had just received a heavenly hug!

In a week filled with drama, obstacles, and distractions, my faith had been bolstered. It would have been easy to lose my faith and patience with God. Instead, He taught me to reach out to Him. I called out. I cried out. It was a make or break sort of week in my walk with Christ.

CHAPTER 7

Déjà Vu

Grady stayed in the hospital for a total of eight days. When we finally got him home, I honestly thought I experienced more joy than after he was born.

The happiness was short-lived.

We kept Grady home from daycare for a full two weeks after his bout with RSV. His pediatrician agreed that would be ample time for recovery and that he'd be healthy enough to return to daycare at that point.

He got sick four days later. We just couldn't keep up with the germs that continued to plague our baby boy. He was home for a long weekend to get better and then back off to daycare.

About a month later, the unthinkable happened. It was early April and one of the first warm days we had that spring. Grady had been home from the hospital for five weeks. I was out mowing the lawn when my wife came out carrying him with a concerned look on her face. I cut the engine and asked her what was wrong. She told me she was worried about his breathing again and wanted to take him to the urgent care. I remember telling her to go right ahead if she wanted to waste her time. I thought the urgent care doctors would just run some expensive tests and send them right back home. I admit that there was a lack of sensitivity and an abundance of frustration in my response.

Thank God mothers are far more nurturing than dads. My wife followed her instincts and ended up taking Grady to the urgent care. By the time I was done mowing the lawn, I had seven text messages from her.

"We're in the back of an ambulance heading to Children's Hospital's ER again," one said. "So call me when you get this."

What? How? This had to be a joke, right? When I reached her, she said the urgent care doctors were not happy with Grady's vital signs, so they transported him directly to the hospital. We had just spent eight days there in the last month. As happy as I was with the care Grady received, it was not a place I wanted to return.

Fire drill time. I called to mobilize the grand-parents, but they were hours away. I knocked on our neighbor's door and interrupted her dinner.

"You're not going to believe this," I said. "Grady is being taken to the ER again."

She dropped everything to come to our house and watch Mackenzie. My poor little girl wanted nothing more than to have a baby brother healthy enough to wrestle.

"Don't take Bubba!" she cried on my way out the door. "I don't want you to take Bubba!"

"Don't worry," I assured her. "Remember we brought him back last time. We'll bring him back again."

I'll never forget that conversation because I wish I had the faith to believe my own words. I cried as I drove the thirty-five minutes to the hospital in Downtown Columbus. It felt like I was in the *Twilight Zone*. Soon another feeling came over me, though. I remembered how God delivered us from the last health scare. I remembered the power He showed then. Somewhere during that drive, the peace that passes all understanding washed over me. I knew God would give me strength through the inevitable hospital stay. Grady's got this and I've got this because God's got us. I arrived at the ER with strength this time. I came prepared to tackle the obstacles our family would face, something I gained from our previous experience.

Grady was once again admitted to the PICU. This time he was diagnosed with human metapneumovirus. To me and you that would be a common cold. To a five-month-old baby whose body is still recovering from RSV, that's really bad news. The BiPAP mask got strapped on his face, oxygen plugged into his nose, and a nasogastric tube went back down his esophagus. What defeat! What agony! What a slap in the face! How could this be happening again?

That's exactly what Satan wanted me to feel.

"Where is this God of yours?" he asked, putting doubt in my mind. "Why would He put your little baby through this again? I thought He loved you."

The only thing I could think to do was pray, to be real with God and show honesty. A few months earlier, I may have used this as an excuse to drink. I certainly would not have used it as a reason to pray. I built up my faith, though, during my fast and Grady's last hospitalization. Now my faith would take over.

I became still. I didn't have any emotion. I wasn't sad. I certainly wasn't happy. I just was. But I wasn't alone. I was with God. God was with me.

The next day in the PICU, they conducted a breathing trial. They removed the BiPAP mask, which is designed to send pressurized oxygen into the depths of your lungs. It was helping Grady breathe deeply. The trial would decide whether they needed to intubate him as they had a month before. I didn't want that for him. Honestly, I didn't want that for me. They took off the mask and said they would be back in twenty minutes. I watched the machine that kept track of his oxygen saturation. The numbers started to fall immediately. I panicked. I didn't want them to intubate him again.

What happened next was Godkward. I gave up all hope of being able to control the situation as I watched Grady's oxygen saturation levels fall. I gave in to the Almighty. I put my hand on Grady's body and prayed out loud.

"God, I trust you. I don't want to trust you. It's hard to trust you. But I do. If it is your will, touch his body. I know you have a purpose for what he is going through, God. Be with us."

> *And we know that God causes*
> *everything to work together for*
> *the good of those who love God*
> *and are called according to His*

purpose for them. (Romans 8:28, NLT)

I turned away from Grady to wipe my tears and grab a pop. I gathered myself, turned back toward my son, and noticed the numbers on the monitor: 86...87...88...89...90...91...92...93...94...95...96. The oxygen saturation steadily climbed. I fell onto the couch and bowed my head. I truly believe it was in that moment that I vowed to always trust in Him.

After the trial was over, the doctors decided to keep him off machines and let him fly solo for a full day. That night I had planned on meeting my life group at church for a volunteer event. We were stuffing twenty thousand Easter eggs for a big annual event the church hosts for the community. I asked my wife if it was still okay if I went. She said yes, as long as I took Mackenzie. No problem. We headed to church, ate candy, and stuffed eggs. We felt normal. I shared what was going on with Grady with the guys in my group. I told them about the struggles but also about the fruits of God's faithfulness.

When we were done stuffing the eggs, I felt something Godkward come over me. I asked my group of guys to join hands and pray. I didn't know why it was awkward. Praying in church shouldn't be awkward, right? But right there in the church entry-way in front of all the other volunteers, we joined hands and bowed our heads. It was a public, powerful, and purposeful prayer. I was taken aback. A group I formed out of my sheer fear of drinking had turned into a circle of trusted, caring friends.

The next day, Grady was released from the hospital directly from the PICU! The doctor even said, "This feels so dirty to release him directly from here, but this kid is not sick."

God is awesome! He is extraordinary. He is exceptional. And if He wants something to be done with, it is done. This was done—finished. At least Grady's role was done. God had used my son's poor health experience to brazen and embolden my heart with his love. He broke me wholly of my own will. He drove me to audibly admit that trusting Him was not easy. He got the result He was looking for: a fully submitted believer. However, His purpose for me was still not fulfilled.

CHAPTER 8

Go Tell It on the Mountain

When we got Grady home, we just couldn't justify putting him back in daycare. It took us a couple of weeks of searching, but we finally found an in-home sitter so Bubba could stay in his "bubble." Paying for a full-time nanny was not cheap, but I had used all of my sick, personal, and vacation days and needed to go back to work. We had hospital bills to pay, after all. Oh, and remember that tiff my wife and I got into over finances during Grady's first hospital stay? That was because we had a huge tax bill due, as well. The combination of those bills would wipe out our savings and leave us with very little cushion.

We were going to have to make some major sacrifices to make ends meet. Ultimately, we decided to put our house on the market and explored moving back to Cleveland where we could find a more appropriately sized house with family nearby. I had swallowed enough pride over the last year to tell you that it does not taste good.

The decision to downsize hurt. We worked really hard for our home and took a lot of pride in it. But it taught me that maybe it is better not to be prideful from the start. God calls us to be humble servants. Jesus Christ Himself was humbled when he willingly went to his own crucifixion. Christians are expected to be Christlike—an impossible feat for the prideful and selfish. That's why Proverbs warns us that pride comes before a fall.

> *Pride goes before destruction, and haughtiness before a fall. (Proverbs 16:18, NLT)*

When I returned to work, I began to share my story. I did this through conversations with coworkers and also sharing some journaling I'd been doing on social media. I was blown away by the responses. I was connecting to people on a whole new level. A colleague even invited me to share my story at his weekly life group from another church.

"You want me to speak at your life group?" I asked, rather surprised by the invitation. "Your circle of Bible friends? The ones you are comfortable with?"

He answered my insecurities by telling me that I have more stories about how I've connected more with the Holy Spirit than anyone he's ever met. He asked me to share some insights with his group that would help them recognize the Holy Spirit in action. I replied with a loud, enthusiastic, Godkward *Yes!*

Speaking at the group went unbelievably well. In fact, they even invited me back the next week. My coworker wouldn't be there. How Godkward would that be? Me attending on my own? But I didn't care. I had a feeling the next meeting would be a blessing and I was excited to go.

The next week, the topic of discussion was heaven. It was that night the Holy Spirit, with some help from my three-year-old, would teach me more about heaven than I ever realized. See we were getting ready to take Mackenzie to Disney World for the first time. It would be a well-deserved vacation and break from the hectic, logistical nightmare our lives had become.

When the room full of adults was asked what they thought heaven would be like, there was a wide range of answers that you might anticipate: streets of gold, no pain, everybody is happy, and see old friends and family. Everyone had their own picture of heaven. Then it hit me. Every time Mackenzie saw a Disney movie or character on TV, she would get beyond excited and say, "We are going there!" As her dad, excited for her to see how awesome it truly is, I always replied, "Mackenzie, you don't even know the half of it."

That's when I heard the Holy Spirit whisper to me. As I sat around talking about the excitement of mansions, pearly gates, and family reunions, I heard God saying, "Adam, you don't even know the half of it." I was filled with excitement! I had taken another Godkward step by attending this group, and it led to a simple yet enthusiastic blessing I would have otherwise missed.

It turned out God had more for me on his Godkward honey-do-list. Next up, I got an email from associate pastor Jake Wirth at Adventure Church asking if I'd be in a Mother's Day video for a service. The filming went great, and the video was successfully humorous and tear-jerking. However, I think God really brought Jake and I together that day so he could hear what God had been doing in my life. I updated him in full and told him I felt like God was really using me. He agreed. In fact, because of what I told him, he gave me my most Godkward invitation to date. He asked me to share my testimony at Unite, an evening the church staff was putting together for their volunteer teams. My reply was a Godkward "I'd totally be game for that. What time?" He gave me the details and asked if I'd prepare a three- to five-minute testimony to share.

"Unite is all about bringing our team together," Jake said. "Your portion would be utilized specifically for encouraging them and showing them the incredible stuff that God is doing through Adventure Church."

"Three to five minutes or thirty-five minutes?" I quipped. Either way, I was in.

He finished by saying, "You're the man, Adam. I would say if you can leverage it to encourage our team and highlight some of the things that God did through AC, that would be amazing. It's easy for our people to lose sight of how important the little things are: greeting, working with the kids, setting up the cafe, leading a life group, etc. If you can somehow do that, it would be huge for all of us."

Wow, I thought. *I only have ten days to pull this off.* I mean you guys are reading this, right? Have any of you gotten this far in three to five minutes? Doubtful.

I was praying, doubting, and praying some more. I kept asking myself what I could possibly say to one hundred plus volunteers. God struck five days early. With time to practice, He gave me this:

Can He Borrow Your Pen?

It would start with a beer.
Party into the night.
Have a few shots.
Maybe get in a fight.

Fight through the hangover.
Fight for my life.
Fight with my friends.
Fight with my wife.
Then my Dad urges
Go to church, but get involved!
Welcome to Adventure Church!
Here's where my story started to evolve.

I put down the booze—
No drinking for me.
I'm starting to get bored!
What can I do for AC (Adventure Church)?

Looking for leaders…
Life groups start in the fall!
"Hmm, I wonder if any
Of these dudes watch football?"

Here ya go, God.
This effort is for You.
I don't know how it's gonna work
But I kinda believe You do.

Started game 1 of the season,
Go Buckeyes, Go!
Now our families are hanging out,
And it's New Year's Eve, whoa!

Five months into sobriety!
I want this feeling to last!
The pastor speaks on Noise,
And I take part in my first fast!

How is this working?
God's talking to me!
He wants me to brag about my
weaknesses!
He wants me to be free!

I've learned we all have trouble.
Our problems can drive us bonkers!
But I've also learned to hang out
daily,
With a God who solves and
conquers!

The leading of a life group
Has become quite a passion!
We even made some tee shirts!
Talk about high fashion!

We are just a group of guys,
Biblically ignorant to say the least.
But we serve a living God who
loves us.
The Dude is quite a beast!

You see He took this shell of a man,
Who liked to party and drink,
And turned him into a humble
volunteer,
With a desire to pray and think!

My hope and prayer remain
That I continue to be curious,
That I'll turn quick to forgiveness,
Instead of becoming furious.

I pray for power!
I pray for peace!
I pray that my will to pray
Will never cease.

To ask Him what my role is
For any given day,
That His plans become mine,
Is how I've begun to pray!

You see it's definitely my story,
But I didn't have to write it.
The Author gave me a fire,
And Adventure Church helped ignite it!

You too have a story,
And if it's starting to become a bore,
Hand the pen back to its Author,
For He has so much more in store!

I felt as though I were on fire for God! I couldn't believe I had been gifted this opportunity to step onto a stage and share my story of sobriety. I could share what God had done in the wake of starting a life group. I texted Jake later that day saying, "You've just poured gasoline on my fire!"

In the weeks following my speech, person after person reached out to me. Whether it was to share their own struggles or the struggles of family members, they encouraged me to press on. They ensured that I would carry on, confirming for me what I had heard God calling me to do: be real, and boast in my weakness. I wasn't connecting with people because I was an incredible poet; I connected with them because I obeyed an incredible God.

> *I know all the things you do, and I have opened a door for you that no one can close. You have little strength, yet you obeyed my word and did not deny me. (Revelation 3:8, NLT)*

CHAPTER 9

Looking Back

On July 24, 2017, I celebrated one year of sobriety! It's best to take this journey one day at a time, but I don't think there is any harm in honoring milestones. It was the toughest year of my life. I gave up drinking, but it wasn't just alcohol to me. Drinking had been my main stress outlet, anxiety reducer, source of courage, and best friend.

Things were going well in my life and my walk with God. The enemy took notice. He threw me so many obstacles during my first year of sobriety, obstacles that I had used as excuses to drink. I had many reasons to celebrate during the year: the birth of my son, a promotion at work, golf outings with the guys, vacations with the family, weddings, and a number of sporting events. And I had reasons to commiserate: my son was hospitalized twice, money was tight, my father-in-law passed away, and our basement flooded. Relationships, finances, and possessions were under attack. Remember Job?

Through God's grace, I learned that those were not reasons to drink anymore. Somewhere along the road, I convinced myself that instead of saying "I've had a rough week. I deserve a beer," it was better to say "I've had a rough week. I don't deserve the consequences a beer would bring." Along the same road, I reconnected with family and friends whom I had hurt. I made a bunch of new friends too. Most importantly, though, I connected with God spiritually. I began living for something other than my own selfish needs. (It has not been an easy lesson to learn.)

I humbly admit that I developed characteristics similar to the Biblical heroes we talked about at the beginning of this story. Like David, I'm ready to face my giant: addiction. Like Peter, I'm willing to give up my own life to follow Jesus. Like Paul, I've found that my purpose is to boast in my weakness because it's the perfect showcase for God's strength. My weaknesses are ever glaring. In AA meetings, I've heard it said that I still have problems, but now they are of a higher quality—meaning abstaining from alcohol has not eliminated my life's problems. However, when I experience a difficult situation or trying time, I am far more equipped to deal with it appropriately now.

I enter Godkward moments with faith. My faith has endured all of the drama from my first year of sobriety. In fact, my faith has been strengthened through the outcomes of those challenges. I used to think faith was for the weak, that it was a crutch for those with nothing else to grasp in times of trouble. Then I became one who seeks God in those troubled times.

I relate to God more and more as a father as I watch my children. I remember watching Grady begin to crawl. He was flat on his belly, arms wide, looking like he was ready to take flight. I think he believed he could fly. My daughter thinks she can fly too. She often soars through the air, whether it be from the back of the couch, the landing of the stairs, or the top of a jungle gym. She's brave that way. However, she never second-guesses her faith in her dad. My children have helped change my opinion of faith. It is not out of weakness that they believe; rather it's their boldness and bravery. Mackenzie will drop into my arms every time she gets stuck. The first jump is always blind trust. One of my colleagues referred to it as "a trust fall for God." It's Godkward the first time you leap, hoping that He will catch you. But when He catches you again and again, it's no longer blind trust: it's wisdom. Mackenzie has learned "Daddy will catch me." That's brave, bold faith. Believing in something she hadn't seen or done before has turned into wise outreach.

When you find yourself inevitably stuck on life's proverbial jungle gym, with obstacles all around, have some courage and put your faith in God. It will undoubtedly feel unnatural. After all, it's hard to believe in something unseen and unheard. God has promised to be faithful, though. Trust that after you take the first Godkward leap of faith into your Heavenly Daddy's arms, you will gain wisdom in knowing He will catch you next time too. Faith is not for the weak, but for the brave. It's not for the optimistic, but for the realist. I still have moments of weakness, but they often make me stronger in situations that would otherwise prove futile. An acronym I like to use for faith is Finally Admitting I'll Take Help. There isn't weakness in asking for help; there is wisdom.

I have also learned that God is not a lifeguard; He's a life vest. He's not always going to dive in and pull you out of rough seas, but He will keep you afloat through the waves. At some point, He'll require you to trust Him. You don't have to wait until you're under duress to accept the kind of peace He has to offer. Yet, we always seem to wait until our chips are down and the odds are stacked against us to call on Him. I've found inspiration, introspection, and information for troubling situations through my journey. Now, I continue my journey with the outlook of "Okay, God. I'm here. What do you want me to learn today? Teach me to use this experience for your will." He has not let me down.

A child learns one way or another not to touch a hot stove. He can obey the guidance of his parents, or he can get burned. God won't spare you from the trials and tribulations of life; He will comfort you through the anxiety and fear if you let Him. I like to remember that without a test, one has no testimony. The more your knees hurt from kneeling, the better your heart will feel as a result. You get to choose how you seek God: in preparation or in desperation. Either way, He will hold you, save you, and teach you—because He loves you!

CHAPTER 10

Encouragement

I hope as you've read my story you have found it relatable. I hope you have found encouragement, too, however small. Most importantly, though, if you take away one thing, know that you can have a personal relationship with the same God David believed in, Peter walked with, and Paul wrote about in the Bible. I feel so undeserving of Jesus's unconditional love, and I find it fascinating that He can and does use anyone, no matter the circumstance. The point is to focus on Him. The Bible says He will establish you!

> *Believe in the Lord your God, and you will be able to stand firm. (2 Chronicles 20:20, NLT)*

We have all been blessed with a skill set uniquely designed by God. He wants a personal relationship with each of us so that He can influence how you use your talents for His glory. I used to think my purpose was to go to work, be a good dad, and be a good husband. Now, I see that my purpose is to serve in any fashion God sees fit, just like Paul wrote in his letter to the Philippians.

> *I once thought these things were valuable, but now I consider them worthless because of what Christ has done. Yes, everything else is worthless when compared with the infinite value of knowing Christ Jesus my Lord. For his sake I have discarded everything else, counting it all as garbage, so that I could gain Christ and become one with him. I no longer count on my own righteousness through obeying the law; rather, I become righteous through faith in Christ. For God's way of making us right with himself depends on faith. I want to know Christ and experi-*

ence the mighty power that raised him from the dead. I want to suffer with him, sharing in his death, so that one way or another I will experience the resurrection from the dead! I don't mean to say that I have already achieved these things or that I have already reached perfection. But I press on to possess that perfection for which Christ Jesus first possessed me. No, dear brothers and sisters, I have not achieved it, but I focus on this one thing: Forgetting the past and looking forward to what lies ahead, I press on to reach the end of the race and receive the heavenly prize for which God, through Christ Jesus, is calling us. (Philippians 3:7–14, NLT)

During my journey, there were a few things that helped me begin recovery and develop this stronger relationship with my Savior: firstly, get to an AA meeting; secondly, develop a daily connection with God; and, finally, find the right church to attend. I understand not everyone considers themselves a "church goer." I've spoken to many people who attended a church, had a bad experience, and then just shoved the whole thing aside. Think about these questions as you consider your experiences. When you eat at a restaurant and have a bad experience (poor atmosphere, food or service), do you quit eating out altogether? Or do you simply try a new restaurant? Chances are you still eat out on occasion.

I would encourage you to take the same approach to church. Perhaps you've tried a church where the atmosphere wasn't up your alley, the spiritual food was lacking, or it just had a poor service. Do yourself a favor; try a different church. Church is about community. You'll certainly find one where you'll enjoy the music and message, if only you continue to look.

I may not be the wisest leader in church history. I may never end up being as holy and inspirational as my grandfather (the pastor of the Baptist church I grew up in). However, I am God's child, and He has a purpose for me. I am alive. I am relatable. I have a story. I believe He wants me to share that passion and story with people. I will "boast in my weakness" to showcase God's strength, just as He says in the Bible.

ADAM McMAHAN AND SEAN JOSEPH

> *This is what the Lord says: Don't let the wise boast in their wisdom, or the powerful boast in their power, or the rich boast in their riches. But those who wish to boast should boast in this alone: that they truly know me and understand that I am the Lord who demonstrates unfailing love and who brings justice and righteousness to the earth and that I delight in these things. I, the Lord, have spoken! (Jeremiah 9:23–24, NLT)*

God is moving. That's not new. He hasn't changed; I have. What started out as an incredibly stupid series of events in a drunken state of mind has led me to be closer to God than ever before. The only Godward thing left to do is to offer to pray with you. For some, maybe this will be the first time you've prayed. For others, perhaps you are regularly meeting with God through prayer. Either way, I want to leave you with a prayer that you can say: No matter the length or strength of your relationship with Christ, I wish you all the very best in your battle with Satan and his army of addictive and anxiety-inducing methods. Don't be afraid to fight the good fight. Don't be afraid to make mistakes. Don't be afraid of running into other problems. God has your back!

> *I have told you all this so that you may have peace in me. Here on earth you will have many trials and sorrows. But take heart, because I have overcome the world. (John 16:33, NLT)*

"Thank you, Heavenly Father, for never giving up on me. Thank You for Your presence, Your power, Your peace. Help me grow in You as You grow in my heart. Encourage me to always seek You. Continue to reveal Yourself and show me how I can do Your will. Give me the courage to follow through with what You would have me do. Amen."

EPILOGUE

The Story Behind Godkward

You guessed it. Writing this book was a little bit Godkward, especially with a coauthor. That's me, Sean Joseph. I'm a former journalist, current teacher nine months of the year, and aspiring author during the summer.

The first time I met Adam, I had no idea that I would spend my next summer break learning about him, writing about him, or writing *as* him. I had been really gung ho about another book project that I wanted to develop into a ministry for Christian teachers in the public schools. I could never get the momentum I needed to get it off the ground, though. I was also starting a life group for families in my church, volunteering with the kids' services, teaching, and, oh yeah, taking care of two beautiful daughters of my own at home. My plate was full.

One Sunday, my wife, Mikki, and I were handing out information about life groups after church with the rest of the leaders. I probably didn't recruit any couples for my group that day, but I joined one. Standing next to me was this boisterous guy with a loud voice and a big, red beard who told me (and everyone else who passed by), "I've never done anything like this before, but my group is going to get together and watch Ohio State football games!"

That was Adam. The more I heard him talking about his group, the more I thought, *Hey, this guy seems like a lot of fun. Maybe I should join his group*. I liked football, after all, and it would be nice to get to know some other guys from church while watching games I would have on anyway. I'll be honest about another motive too: I needed more masculinity in my life. I was surrounded by girls at home (even the dog), and I was one of the only male employees at the elementary school where I taught. I needed this.

I signed up and showed up, on time, for the first game. You may recall from Adam's story that this was the game with the long weather delay. So I showed up to this guy's house for the first time and sat in his basement waiting for the game to start and trying to convince myself that it wasn't really awkward. I didn't know what to do with myself, so I got up to get another piece of pizza and a drink. When I opened the fridge, it was stocked with soda and water bottles. Thinking back to this moment, I blame my awkward need to keep a conversation going for what happened next.

"Hey, man," I say, trying to make innocent small talk and inject some humor. "Where's the beer?"

All chatter in the room stops—awkward silence.

"We're watching football, right?"

Jaws drop.

"I don't remember the last time I watched a Buckeyes game without beer!"

Wide eyes shoot sideway glances across the room.

I knew I had said something wrong, but I had just met Adam. I had no idea he had quit drinking less than two months prior. I wouldn't find out that night, either, though apparently the other two guys in the room knew, hence the stunned looks and awkward silence.

I'll give Adam credit here. He didn't know me well enough to tell me his story, and that's understandable. He also didn't kick me out of his house (though apparently my status as a group member came into question later). He defused the situation with some witty line that put everyone back at ease.

I can't remember what Adam said in response to my ignorance, but I do remember that he made it clear he'd done some heavy drinking in his life and that this group would not. That's why I wasn't too surprised when he told me he attended AA the next time I saw him (yes, I was actually invited back!). I immediately thought back to my awkward comment, gathered my words, and apologized for making things uncomfortable. He brushed it off, and we moved on to other topics. That was possibly the first Godkward moment that led to writing this book. After all, if he hadn't invited me back, or if he held a grudge, I would never have realized how great a story he had to tell.

Little by little, as fall turned into winter and spring, I learned about parts of Adam's journey to sobriety and the events that he'd gone through since. Adam coined the term Godkward during one life group meeting as he told us about speaking in front of people at church. "Sounds like a good book title," he joked. "Maybe I'll write one."

A lightbulb went on in my head. *This guy has a great story to tell*, I thought. It's got ups and downs and twists and turns. It has moments that make you want to stand up and clap and moments where you want to bang your head against the wall. There are some events in his story that make you want to give him a hug and others when you want to slap him upside the head. I didn't say anything about it that night, but when I got home I couldn't stop thinking about his story. The next morning, I felt God had put it on my heart to ask him about partnering up to write his story. I was at a loss for next steps when it came to my other book. Now, I believe God put that on hold for a reason. I was looking for something to write about when summer started in a few short weeks. So after praying about it on my way to work that morning, I sent my first Godkward text message.

"Hey man, I've been thinking a lot about your Godkward book idea. I feel like God wants me to help you write it."

He could have said "No, that's weird" or "I don't need your help writing my own story." But he didn't. We decided to explore the idea and ultimately to make Godkward happen. And it was very Godkward!

I started by reading some journals Adam wrote about how his journey to sobriety started and Grady's hospitalization. I knew He had a powerful story that could help a lot of people fighting battles of recovery, but I needed to know more. The journalist in me took over and wrote a list of ten to fifteen questions for him to answer probing deeper into the story. Why did your wife give you an ultimatum? How had you embarrassed her? Why are you on probation? It was deep stuff, and I was nervous I'd scare him off with such personal questions.

He Godkwardly answered everything in full detail. He was so honest that I remember thinking, *If I did all of this stuff, my wife would have killed me!* (Thank you, Lindsey, for sparing your husband.) I started writing, slowly at first. Every time I picked up my pen, I imagined that Adam wouldn't like it, that it would make Lindsey mad, or that I just wasn't a good writer. Now, I realize the devil was trying to tell me the book wouldn't go anywhere anyway. Satan didn't want the book to be written because he didn't want lives to be changed or people to become closer to God. The Holy Spirit gave me the strength to power through. I'd sneak in writing time whenever I could during my daughters' naps or after they went to bed. I eventually got to typing up drafts of what would become the first two chapters of this book and emailed them off to Adam. If he didn't like them, Godkward would probably be dead in the water, or my part in it at least.

The feedback I received from Adam kept me going. He was shocked that what started out as a couple of journal entries was starting to sound like an actual book. To be honest, so was I! On top of that, his wife actually agreed and wanted us to keep writing. That was a big deal, because I knew if it didn't have spousal approval, there was no sense in moving forward. They both said it was a very Godkward read, of course. The book brought back some raw emotion from events that led to Adam's sobriety. It was also strange for both of us to read what I wrote in first person—using his words and his point of view. Imagine someone else saying I, and that I is you.

As we plodded along in the drafting process, I felt myself being drawn closer to God. Even though I had not been through any similar battles, I was amazed by how a regular guy can be so in tune with the Holy Spirit working in his life. I started noticing Godkward moments in my own life and being able to respond to them enthusiastically. This process has taught me that writing isn't just a hobby I enjoy; perhaps it is God's purpose for my life. I can serve His Kingdom through writing if I listen for inspiration from God. I hope you get as much out of reading this as I did from writing.

I won't bore you with the rest of the writing process, but I do want to say thanks for some people that helped make this a reality. First, thank you Adam (and the whole McMahan family) for letting me tell your story. I'd also like to thank my daughters, Julia and Lydia, for having rest time that allowed me to write this book and still pack our summer days with trips to the zoo, pool, and park. Finally, I need to thank my wife, Mikki, for her support because I know giving me the time to write really cut into my summer honey-do-list. Thank you, God, for putting the words on these pages, and bless those who read them!

ABOUT THE AUTHORS

 Adam McMahan is married to his wife, Lindsey, with whom he has two children, Mackenzie and Grady. Adam lives just outside of Columbus, Ohio, where he spends his work week as a banker. He enjoys writing, golfing, Cleveland sports teams, and leading his life group "First and Faith" at Adventure Church in Lewis Center, Ohio. He is a recovering alcoholic who is finding new purpose in sharing the story of his battle with addiction in an effort to help those in need of recovery find purpose in Christ.

Sean Joseph is married to his wife, Mikki, and has two daughters, Julia and Lydia. He is a middle school teacher in Columbus, Ohio. He enjoys writing, running, gardening, leading a family life group, and working with the kids at Adventure Church. Sean met Adam through a Godkward men's  life group which resulted in him finding his purpose in faith-based writing and publishing his first book!